## A New True Book

# HOW A BOOK
# IS MADE

### By Carol Greene

CHILDRENS PRESS ®

CHICAGO

PHOTO CREDITS

Journalism Services:
© Joseph Jacobson—2
© Scott Wanner—cover, 7, 10, 12, 15, 19,
20, 21, 22 (3 photos), 23, 25 (2 photos), 26,
27, 28 (2 photos), 29, 30 (2 photos), 31, 32,
33, 34, 35 (2 photos), 36, 37, 38, 41
(2 photos), 42 (2 photos), 43 (left)
© Harvey Moshman—40

© Margaret Cooper—4, 8

Image Finders:
© R. Flanagan—43 (right), 44

Cameramann International Ltd—44 (top
right, bottom left & right)

Artwork by Tom Dunnington—6

Cover: Printer pulls a sheet
        from the printing press

686
G    $9.95
1-91

Library of Congress Cataloging-in-Publication Data

Greene, Carol.
    How a book is made / by Carol Greene.
        p.      cm. — (A New true book)
    Includes index.
    Summary: Presents the steps taken by a manuscript
as it is transformed into a printed book.
    ISBN 0-516-01216-9
    1.  Books—Juvenile literature.   2.  Book industries
and trade—Juvenile literature.   3.  Publishers and
publishing—Juvenile literature.   4.  Printing—
Juvenile literature. [1.  Books.   2.  Book industries
and trade.   3.  Publishers and
publishing.   4.  Printing.]  I.  Title.
Z116.A2G73   1988                          87-33788
686—dc19                                   CIP
                                           AC

# TABLE OF CONTENTS

Carol Greene is the author of this book
and many other books for young readers.

# FROM IDEA
# TO MANUSCRIPT

Each book begins with an idea in the writer's mind. The idea can come from many places. Sometimes the writer imagines it or reads something that suggests it.

It might be an idea about a real person, place, or thing. Mother Teresa. England. Robots. Then it is an idea for a nonfiction book.

Illustration from *A Computer Went-A-Courting* written by Carol Greene and illustrated by Tom Dunnington.

It might be an idea for an invented story. What if a computer fell in love with a mouse? What if an elephant became a spy? Then it is an idea for a fiction book.

Writers think about their ideas. They may do

research in libraries. When was Mother Teresa born? Sometimes they talk to experts. How does a robot work? Writers want their facts to be correct.

Some writers use a pen or pencil. Others use a typewriter or word processor.

This author types her manuscript on a word processor in an office.

Carol Greene works in an office at home.

One writer may work at home. Another may rent an office. Some work better in the morning. Others work best at night.

Most writers rewrite their books several times. When they think their book is ready, they mail it to a publisher.

# DECISIONS

An editor at the publishing house will read the manuscript. Editors read many manuscripts each year. They decide which ones will make good books.

Is there something new about this manuscript? Will people want to read it? Will they buy it? Editors must answer these questions.

An editor (right) presents a book to the publisher (left) and the
sales manager of paperback books (center).

If the editor thinks the
book is good, he or she
presents the idea to the
publisher. Together they
decide whether or not their
company should publish it.

If the decision is no, the editor sends the manuscript back to the writer.

If the decision is yes, the editor writes or calls the writer.

The editor has read the manuscript carefully. He or she may see ways the writer can make it better.

An editor (left) asks an author to rewrite part of her manuscript.

The editor and writer work together to make the book better.

When the problems are solved, the editor sends the writer a contract. This contract is a legal promise. The publisher promises to publish the book and to pay the writer.

The publisher may pay one lump sum of money. This is called a fee or an outright purchase.

Sometimes the publisher pays the author some money for each copy sold. This is called a royalty.

Publishers usually send the writer a check before the book is published. This is called an advance.

# FROM EDITOR
# TO DESIGNER

Now the editor must talk to people in the sales department and the art department. Together they must decide what size the book will be. If it needs pictures, who will draw them? If it needs photographs, who will get them?

After these decisions are made, the editor goes back to work on the manuscript.

An editor (left) works with a photo researcher (middle) and the vice president of sales and marketing (right).

The editor prepares the material at the front and back of the book too. There must be at least one page for the title. It usually includes the author's name, the artist's

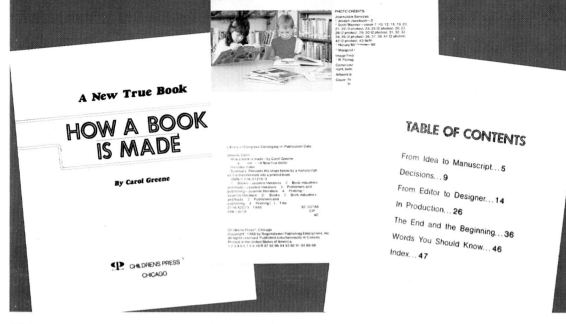

A New True Book

HOW A BOOK IS MADE

By Carol Greene

CP CHILDRENS PRESS
CHICAGO

All books must have a title page (left) and a copyright page (center). Some books have a table of contents (right).

name, and the publisher's name.

There must be a page for the copyright notice. This notice warns people that it is against the law to copy the book.

The Library of Congress Cataloging-in-Publication

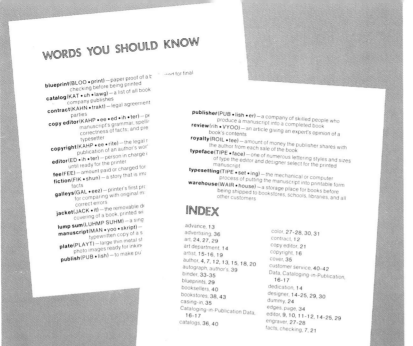

Many books
have a glossary,
a listing of
words the reader
should know,
and an index.

Data often appears on the
copyright page. It helps
librarians know where to
put the book.

The book may also have
a dedication page and a
table of contents in the
front. In the back may be
a glossary and an index.

Sometimes information about the author and the artist appears in the back of the book. Or it can appear on the book's jacket. The editor makes sure all this material is complete.

Then the designer takes over. Designers decide which typeface to use. How big should the type be?

The designer decides how the book should look.

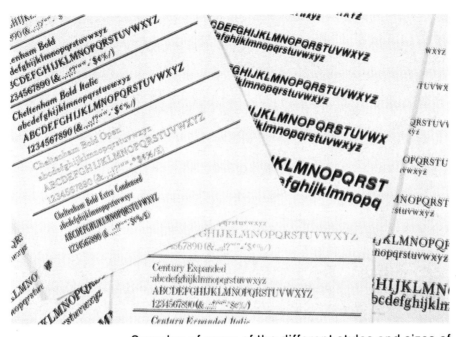

Samples of some of the different styles and sizes of type. Typesetters measure type size in points. This book is set in 22 point Helvetica Light.

If the book needs pictures, the designer hires an artist. The artist may be paid a fee or a royalty.

The designer and the artist decide how the pictures should look. The pictures must always agree

An artist
works on an
illustration
for a
picture book.

with the author's words.

Artists may have to do research. If a story is set during the Civil War, the buildings and clothes should look right for that time.

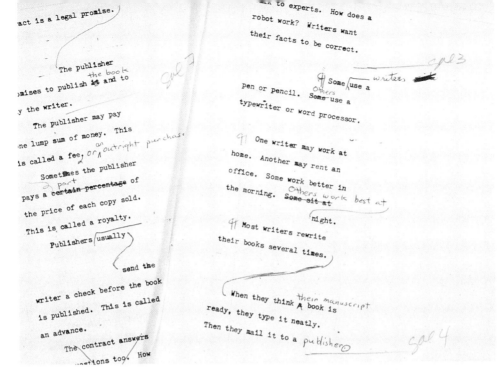

Sample of a copyedited manuscript

Meanwhile, the copy editor checks the manuscript to make sure spelling and punctuation are correct. Copy editors also check facts. For example, was Mother Teresa really born in 1910?

Typesetters (above) use computers to set type.
The type is printed in long sheets called galleys.

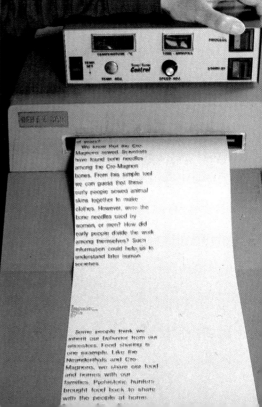

An editor proofreads the galleys for errors.

Then the designer sends
the copyedited manuscript
to the typesetter. At first
the type is printed on long
sheets of paper. These are
called galley proofs. Many
people, including the
writer, read the galleys to
make sure there are no

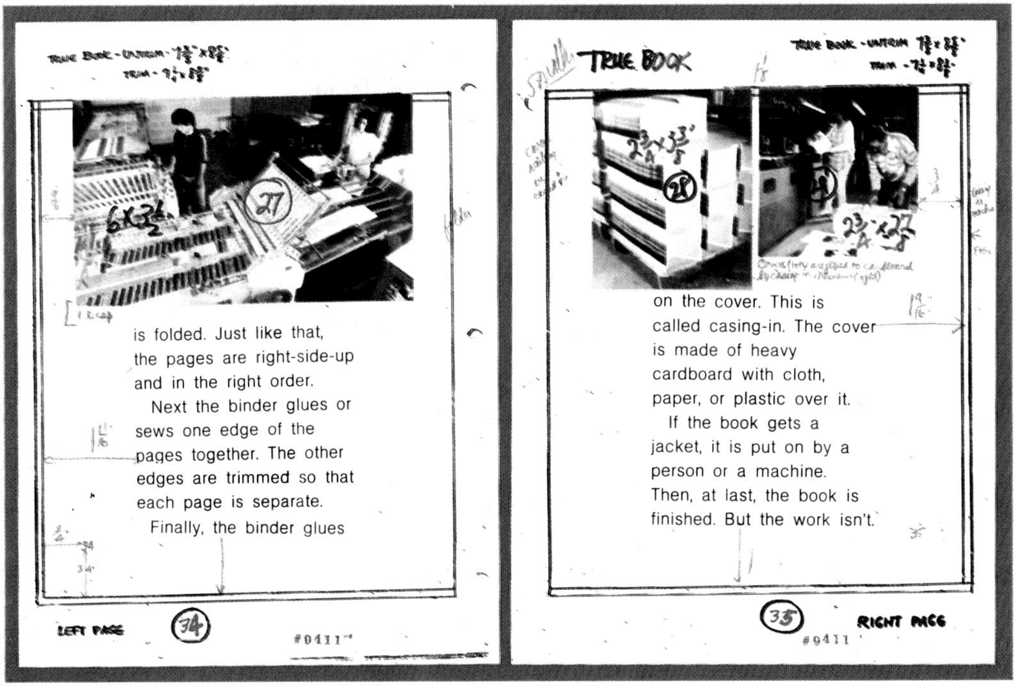
TRUE BOOK
is folded. Just like that, the pages are right-side-up and in the right order.
Next the binder glues or sews one edge of the pages together. The other edges are trimmed so that each page is separate.
Finally, the binder glues
LEFT PAGE
34
#0411
on the cover. This is called casing-in. The cover is made of heavy cardboard with cloth, paper, or plastic over it.
If the book gets a jacket, it is put on by a person or a machine. Then, at last, the book is finished. But the work isn't.
35
RIGHT PAGE
#0411
The designer uses the galleys to make a layout or dummy book.

mistakes. This is called proofreading.

The designer uses the galley proofs to make a layout or dummy book. He or she shows exactly where the type and the art should be placed on each page.

Keyliners paste the type onto boards. They must make sure that each line of type is straight and positioned where the designer wants it.

The typesetter follows the designer's layout and pastes the proofread type onto large boards. These are called keylines.

When the designer and the editor okay the typesetter's work, the book is ready to go into production.

# IN PRODUCTION

Production people keep track of what happens next. They choose and buy paper and decide who will do each job. They make

The production manager checks a roll of paper at the printer.

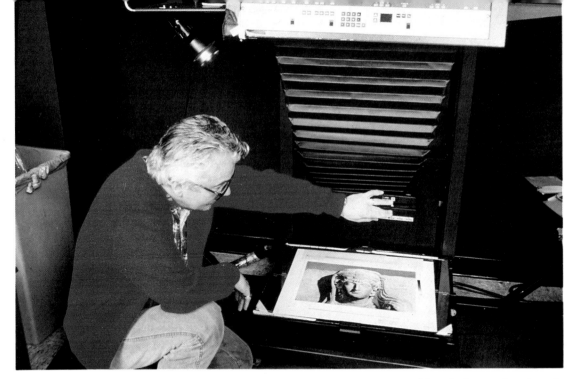

Huge cameras are used to photograph artwork.

sure each job gets done on time.

Engravers are hired. Engravers photograph the type and the art to make film.

If the book has color pictures, the engraver must

27

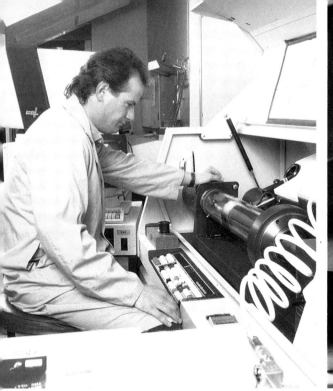

Engraver (left) uses a computer to separate art into four pieces of film. Each piece of film must be checked.

make a separate film for each color. Most color pictures are made from four pieces of film—yellow, red, blue, and black.

After the films are made, paper proofs, often called

An editor reads the blueprints carefully.

blueprints, are made. The
designer and the editor
read the blueprints
carefully.

The designer has also
seen proofs of the art in

A designer (left) checks the original 35mm slide against
a color proof. A pressman (right) puts a plate on a press.

color. If the color proofs
are not good, the designer
makes corrections. If the
blueprints and the color
proofs are correct, the book
is ready to be printed.

This press prints in four colors—yellow, red, blue, and black. A plate is made for each color.

The production department sends the films to the printer. The printer uses the film to make plates for the presses. One plate is made for each color of ink— yellow, red, blue, black.

A pressman pulls a sheet from the press.

When the plates are made, the presses begin to roll. The book is printed on huge sheets.

A ninety-six page book can be printed on one sheet. But it will look strange. Pages are not in

The foreman (right) and a pressman examine the press sheet to make sure the ink is spread evenly over the paper and that the colors are right.

order. Some are upside-down.

The production manager has planned how the pages must be printed on the sheet. When they get to the binder, each sheet

The press sheets are folded by machine at the bindery.

is folded. Just like that,
the pages are right-side-up
and in the right order.

Next the binder glues or
sews one edge of the
pages together. The other
edges are trimmed so that
each page is separate.
Finally, the binder glues

A casing-in machine attaches the covers (left) to the book bodies (above).

on the cover. This is
called casing-in. The cover
is made of heavy
cardboard with cloth,
paper, or plastic over it.

If the book gets a
jacket, it is put on by a
person or a machine.
Then, at last, the book is
finished. But the work isn't.

The advertising manager and the general manager plan a book promotion campaign.

# THE END AND THE BEGINNING

Now people must sell the book.

Advertising people write ads and mail out catalogs.

Catalogs and brochures tell librarians about all the new books published by Childrens Press.

Sales representatives bring new books to their customers.

Sales representatives visit bookstores, schools, and libraries.

Authors may help sell their books too. Some talk to children in schools or to groups of adults. They might appear on radio or TV. Some autograph their books at stores.

Publishers also send their new books to newspapers and magazines. There the books are given to experts who review them. A review tells whether a book is good or bad and why. Sometimes experts don't agree about this.

Librarians buy the books that the people who use their library need and want.

Librarians and booksellers listen to sales representatives, look at catalogs or sample books, and read reviews. Then they decide whether or not to order.

At the publishing house, customer service people take care of the orders. They have books shipped

A sales representative (above) shows a book to a buyer in a bookstore. Customer service representatives (below) answer questions and make sure that the book orders are correct.

Books are stored in bins by stock numbers. The workers
pack each order into boxes for shipment to the customer.

from the warehouse and
they mail bills. They
handle problems, such as
damaged books or lost
shipments.

Now you know how books are made. When you go to the library and read a wonderful book, remember all the people who worked very hard to get that book into your hands.

At last the book sits on a bookstore or library shelf. Someone comes in who wants to read it. Home goes the book and the reader opens it.

Books open up a world of adventure.

Many things can happen then. One reader may fly away to England. Another may think of ways to be like Mother Teresa. One reader may laugh at the computer and the mouse. Another may decide to build a robot.

The book is finished. But the adventures have just begun!

# WORDS YOU SHOULD KNOW

**blueprint**(BLOO • print) —paper proof of a book used for final checking before being printed

**catalog**(KAT • uh • lawg) —a list of all books, with prices, that the company publishes

**contract**(KAHN • trakt) —legal agreement between two or more parties

**copy editor**(KAHP • ee • ed • ih • ter) —person who checks manuscript's grammar, spelling, punctuation and correctness of facts; and prepares manuscript for typesetter

**copyright**(KAHP • ee • rite) —the legal right granted for exclusive publication of an author's work

**editor**(ED • ih • ter) —person in charge of a manuscript's progress until ready for the printer

**fee**(FEE) —amount paid or charged for a service

**fiction**(FIK • shun) —a story that is imagined, not based on real facts

**galleys**(GAL • eez) —printer's first proof of type used by the editor for comparing with original manuscript copy to detect and correct errors

**jacket**(JACK • it) —the removable decorative and protective paper covering of a book, printed with title, author, and publisher

**lump sum**(LUHMP SUHM) —a single payment

**manuscript**(MAN • yoo • skript) —an author's handwritten or typewritten copy of a story

**plate**(PLAYT) —large thin metal sheet impressed with the type and photo images ready for inking and printing

**publish**(PUB • lish) —to make public

**publisher**(PUB • lish • er) — a company of skilled people who
produce a manuscript into a completed book

**review**(rih • VYOO) — an article giving an expert's opinion of a
book's contents

**royalty**(ROIL • tee) — amount of money the publisher shares with
the author from each sale of the book

**typeface**(TIPE • face) — one of numerous lettering styles and sizes
of type the editor and designer select for the printed
manuscript

**typesetting**(TIPE • set • ing) — the mechanical or computer
process of putting the manuscript into printable form

**warehouse**(WAIR • house) — a storage place for books before
being shipped to bookstores, schools, libraries, and all
other customers

# INDEX

## About the Author

Carol Greene has degrees in English Literature and Musicology. She has worked in international exchange programs, as an editor, and as a teacher. She now lives in St. Louis, Missouri, and writes full time. She has published over seventy books, most of them for children.